THE G. SCHIRMER INSTRUM

MW01130092

THE
HORN
COLLECTION

12 PIECES
BY 12 COMPOSERS

WITH TWO COMPANION CDs

ISBN: 978-1-4234-0658-7

G. SCHIRMER, *Inc.*

DISTRIBUTED BY

HAL•LEONARD®
CORPORATION
7777 W. BLUEMOUND RD. P.O. BOX 13819 MILWAUKEE, WI 53213

www.schirmer.com
www.halleonard.com

CONTENTS

ABOUT THE MUSIC

LUDWIG VAN BEETHOVEN

Austrian composer. Born in Bonn, December 17, 1770.
Died in Vienna, March 26, 1827.

German Dance

The great Beethoven wrote music in all of the important genres, composing monumental
symphonies, piano sonatas, string quartets, concertos, and solo sonatas. Among his smaller
works are a number of German Dances for various combinations of instruments. This German
Dance was transcribed and arranged for horn and piano by Mason Jones.

JOHANNES BRAHMS

German composer. Born in Hamburg, May 7, 1833.
Died in Vienna, April 3, 1897.

Scherzo
from Serenade No. 1 in D Major, Op. 11, No. 2

Brahms is considered Beethoven's successor in the areas of the symphony and chamber music.
He was a fierce critic of his own music, often refusing to publish works that he deemed
inferior. He originally wrote this Serenade (1857-58) for chamber ensemble, but later scored
it for full orchestra. The first performance of the orchestral transcription took place in
Hanover on March 3, 1860. This transcription of the Scherzo was created by Mason Jones.

LUIGI CHERUBINI

Italian composer. Born in Florence, September, 1760.
Died in Paris, March 15, 1842.

Sonata No. 1
from Two Sonatas (Concert Etudes) for French Horn and String Orchestra

Luigi Cherubini spent much of his career in France, where he was a popular composer of opera
and religious music. His career spanned the end of the classical period and the beginning of
the romantic period; his music shows elements of both stylistic trends. Highly admired by his
contemporaries, Beethoven called Cherubini "the greatest living composer." Cherubini wrote
two sonatas for horn and string orchestra in 1804, calling them etudes or studies. Sonatas are
almost always for solo instruments and piano, or piano; sonatas with orchestra are very rare.
The first sonata of the pair consists of a single movement.

Barry Tuckwell, considered the greatest horn player of his generation, created this edition of
Cherubini's Sonata No. 1.

ENRIQUE GRANADOS
Catalan composer. Born in Lérida, July 27, 1867.
Died at sea in the English Channel, March 24, 1916.

Orientale
from *12 Danzas españolas,* Vol. 1, No. 3

Granados, a Spanish composer and accomplished pianist, is remembered for a few
significant compositions: his *Danzas españolas,* his opera *María del Carmen,* and his opera
Goyescas. Granados completed his *12 Danzas españolas* in 1890. Some of the dance
movements have been transcribed frequently for other instruments, including "Orientale."
Kazimierz Machala created this transcription for horn and piano. Granados' last opera,
Goyescas, was premiered by the Metropolitan Opera in New York in 1916. Its success resulted
in an invitation to perform for President Wilson which delayed the planned return to Spain.
On the alternate route back to Europe, the ship on which Granados traveled was torpedoed
in the English Channel. He was rescued but dove back into the sea to save his wife. Neither
survived. His music, which is often described as having a spontaneous quality, evokes the
colors and atmosphere of his native Spain.

GEORGE FRIDERIC HANDEL
German-English composer. Born in Halle, February 23, 1685.
Died in London, April 14, 1759.

I See a Huntsman
(Va tacito e nascosto)
from the opera *Giulio Cesare in Egitto*

After a brief time in Italy as a young man, Handel spent his career in England, where he
primarily composed opera and oratorio. One of the most important composers of the Baroque
period, he was enormously famous and successful during his lifetime. Handel wrote dozens of
operas in the Italian Baroque style. Handel was a master of the da capo aria, which consisted
of three sections: a first section (A), a contrasting section (B) and a repeat of the first section
decorated with ornaments added by the performer (A'). *Giulio Cesare in Egitto (Julius Caesar
in Egypt)* was premiered in London in 1724. In the plot of the opera, Julius Caesar in a power
struggle for the Roman Empire with Pompey, travels to Alexandria to confront him. Tolomeo
and his sister Cleopatra, rulers of Egypt, have Pompey murdered. Caesar voices his disgust of
the murder to Tolomeo. After this confrontation, Caesar is alone to contemplate death in
this aria, a metaphor of the hunter's silent stalking of his prey. "I See a Huntsman" is an
arrangement of the aria, "Va tacito e nascosto," or "He goes quietly and in secret" by
Mason Jones.

WOLFGANG AMADEUS MOZART
Austrian composer. Born in Salzburg, January 27, 1756.
Died in Vienna, December 5, 1791.

Romanze
second movement from Horn Concerto No. 3 in E-flat Major, K. 447

The natural horn of Mozart's day did not include valves. The players controlled pitch
exclusively by the movement of their lips and hand-stopping. Mozart completed his third
concerto for horn in Vienna around 1787, though he wrote the first movements much earlier.

Nearly all of Mozart's horn music, including this concerto, was written for his friend Joseph
Leutgeb (1745-1811), the horn player for the archbishop's court in Salzburg. Leutgeb was the
first horn player to concertize in Europe using the newly developed hand-stopping technique.
In 1777, he inherited a cheese shop in Vienna and moved there with the financial assistance
of Leopold Mozart. When Wolfgang later moved to Vienna, they continued their friendship.
Many of Mozart's manuscripts include comments next to the horn part poking fun at Leutgeb.
Mozart, before his death, in letters to his wife, mentions that for financial reasons he has had
to let the maid go and has gone to stay with Leutgeb. As Mozart became ever weaker, Leutgeb
even helped him to dress.

MODEST MUSSORGSKY
Russian composer. Born in Karevo, March 21, 1839.
Died in St. Petersburg, March 28, 1881.

The Song of Khivria
from the opera *Sorochintsy Fair*

Modest Mussorgsky (pronounced muh-ZORG-skee) was a self-taught composer who was not
well known during his lifetime, but is now considered a master composer. His most famous
works include the colorful and dramatic opera *Boris Godunov*, the orchestral song cycle
Songs and Dances of Death, the symphonic poem *Night on Bald Mountain*, and the piano
suite *Pictures at an Exhibition*. His contemporary, Rimsky-Korsakov (1844-1908), edited,
orchestrated, and revised many of Mussorgsky's works after the composer's death, ironing
out Mussorgsky's idiosyncrasies. In the 20th Century, Mussorgsky's distinctive original versions
are more often performed.

The "Song of Khivria" appears in Mussorgsky's lesser-known opera, *Sorochintsy Fair*. Mason
Jones created this arrangement of the aria for horn and piano.

GIACOMO PUCCINI

Italian composer. Born in Lucca, December 22, 1858.
Died in Brussels, November 29, 1924.

Parisian Waltz
(Quando men vo)
from the opera *La bohème*

Puccini's operas *La bohème*, *Madama Butterfly*, and *Tosca* are among the most frequently performed in opera houses around the world today. *La bohème*, premiered in 1896, is about poor artists in Paris, and is probably the most popular opera in the repertory. In the second act, a group of young Parisians are out on the town celebrating Christmas Eve when the charming Musetta, former lover of the painter Marcello, arrives on the scene. She causes quite a disturbance attempting to make Marcello jealous as she sings her waltz "Quando men vo" wherein she describes the way everyone stares at her in adoration when she walks alone in the street.

HENRY PURCELL

English composer. Born in London, 1659.
Died in London, November 21, 1695.

I Attempt from Love's Sickness to Fly
from the semi-opera *The Indian Queen*

Purcell (pronounced PUHR-suhl) was the greatest English Baroque composer, and considered the most important composer of that nationality until the 20th century. Besides a great deal of church music and ceremonial music for the royal court, Purcell composed an enormous amount of incidental theater music. Theater life in London during the Restoration period, the decades following 1660 when the monarchy was restored after the English civil war, greatly favored spoken drama. This preference was in reaction to a ban on theater for the previous 20 years. Opera had not yet come into favor in London. As a result, none was composed for the professional stage. Thus the existence of "semi-operas," such as Purcell's *The Indian Queen*, with spoken dialogue heavily interspersed with music. *The Indian Queen*, with a text by the great poets John Dryden (1631-1700) and Sir Robert Howard (1626-1698), first appeared in London in 1695. The historically impossible plot involves a war between the Peruvian Incas and the Mexican Aztecs. "I Attempt from Love's Sickness to Fly," is the Aztec queen's expression of unrequited love. This arrangement by Mason Jones is a minuet in the form of a rondo.

CAMILLE SAINT-SAËNS

French composer. Born in Paris, October 9, 1835.
Died in Algiers, December 16, 1921.

Romance for Horn (or Cello) and Orchestra
Op. 36

Saint-Saëns once stated, "He who does not get absolute pleasure from a simple series of well-constructed chords, beautiful only in their arrangement, is not really fond of music." Camille Saint-Saëns was a prolific composer, writing pieces in virtually every genre. He was a popular composer during his lifetime, and is remembered today for orchestral works such as *Le carnaval des animaux (The Carnival of the Animals)*, his opera *Samson et Dalila*, and works for solo instruments with orchestra. In 1874 he completed the "Romance," Op. 36, for horn (or cello) and orchestra.

ROBERT SCHUMANN

German composer. Born in Zwickau, June 8, 1810.
Died in Endenich, July 29, 1856.

Reverie
(Träumerei)
from *Scenes from Childhood (Kinderscenen)*, Op. 15, No. 7

Besides composing symphonies, chamber works, and many songs, Schumann excelled in creating many jewel-like miniatures for piano that express a poetic mood or image. This piece, originally for piano, is from *Kinderscenen*, a collection of 13 short pieces Schumann wrote in 1838.

Louis Stout, Sr. (1924-2005), a famous horn player, created this transcription of Schumann's *Träumerei*. In addition to his teaching positions, Stout performed with numerous major orchestras.

ALEXANDER SCRIABIN

Russian composer. Born in Moscow, January 6, 1872.
Died in Moscow, April 27, 1915.

Romance for Horn and Piano

Alexander Scriabin (pronounced skree-AH-bin) was an influential Russian composer and pianist. He took a philosophical approach to composition that bordered on mysticism. His interests in the metaphysical were considered eccentric. Scriabin believed that each pitch had a corresponding color, and that one sensory experience triggered another. He is best remembered for his orchestral works and numerous compositions for the piano. As an adult, Scriabin – who was a brilliant pianist – performed only his own compositions in public. He wrote a handful of chamber compositions, including the Romance for horn and piano, completed in 1890.

A NOTE ON ARTICULATION AND PHRASING
Articulation and phrasing decisions are often left up to the performer or teacher, particularly in Baroque music, based on ability level, as well as interpretation. We have included minimal articulation and phrasing markings in the music, which should be treated as suggestions, and not necessarily the only solution for a given passage. The artist on the recording uses articulations and phrasings that do not always reflect the printed markings, but demonstrate his personal musical ideas for the repertoire. We encourage you to experiment with different approaches that convey the music for you and your abilities.

German Dance

Transcribed by Mason Jones

Ludwig van Beethoven
(1770–1827)

Scherzo
from Serenade No. 1 in D Major, Op. 11, No. 2

Transcribed by Mason Jones

Johannes Brahms
(1833–1897)

Sonata No. 1
from Two Sonatas (Concert Etudes) for French Horn and String Orchestra

Transcribed by Barry Tuckwell

Luigi Cherubini
(1760–1842)

Orientale

from *12 Danzas españolas*, Vol. 1, No. 3

Transcribed by Kazimierz Machala

Enrique Granados
(1867–1916)

I See a Huntsman

(Va tacito e nascosto)

from the opera *Giulio Cesare in Egitto*

Transcribed by Mason Jones

George Frideric Handel
(1685–1759)

22

Romanze

second movement from Horn Concerto No. 3 in E-flat Major, K. 447

Wolfgang Amadeus Mozart
(1756–1791)

The Song of Khivria

from the opera *Sorochintsy Fair*

Transcribed by Mason Jones

Modest Mussorgsky
(1839–1881)

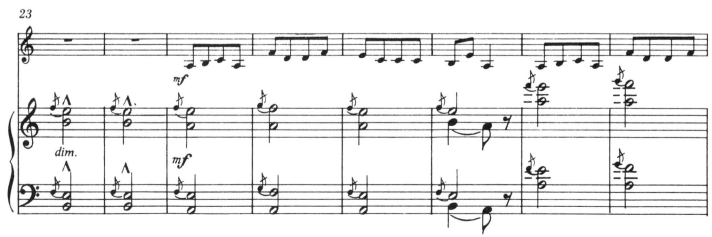

32

Parisian Waltz
(Quando men vo)
from the opera *La bohème*

Transcribed by Hansel Powell

Giacomo Puccini
(1858–1924)

20
rit. molto
mp
p
a tempo
molto rall.
25
rit.
a tempo
poco rall.
29
a tempo
mf
8va
cresc.
rit. molto
33
a tempo
f espansivo
rall.
p

I Attempt from Love's Sickness to Fly

from the semi-opera *The Indian Queen*

Arranged by Mason Jones

Henry Purcell
(1659–1695)

Romance for Horn (or Cello) and Orchestra
Op. 36

Camille Saint-Saëns
(1835–1921)

Reverie

(Träumerei)

from *Scenes from Childhood* (*Kinderscenen*), Op. 15, No. 7

Transcribed by Louis Stout

(M.M. ♩ =54)
Andante

Robert Schumann
(1810–1856)

Romance for Horn and Piano

Alexander Scriabin
(1872–1915)

ABOUT THE PERFORMERS

Bernhard Scully, horn

Horn soloist Bernhard Scully has been described as among the elite musicians of his generation, both as a performer and a pedagogue. He is currently the Professor of Horn at the University of Illinois at Urbana-Champaign. There he is a member of the Illinois Brass Quintet, co-director of the Orchestral Repertoire Class, and director of the Audition Preparation Class. He is currently on the faculty of the Kendall Betts Horn Camp and the Rafael Mendez Brass Institute as a member of the Summit Brass, and has been on the faculty of the Music Academy of the West and the Eastman School of Music. In 2011, Bernhard began the first ever Illinois Summer Youth Music Horn Week at the University of Illinois at Urbana-Champaign for pre-college horn players.

Previously Bernhard was a member of the Canadian Brass. With the group he performed the world over, recorded numerous CDs, and starred in a top-ranked music video. As a featured artist in the quintet he shared the stage and soloed with some of the world's greatest symphony orchestras such as the New York Philharmonic, Philadelphia Orchestra, Detroit Symphony, and Toronto Symphony, National Arts Centre Orchestra, New Jersey Symphony, Vancouver Symphony, among many others. He gave master classes worldwide to thousands of students at many of the world's premiere music schools.

As a soloist, he is a regular featured artist at universities, workshops, conventions, and with prominent ensembles. Bernhard has recorded *The G. Schirmer Instrumental Library Horn Collection*, Volumes 1-3 published by Hal Leonard, which includes much of the standard literature for horn and piano. His CD entitled, *Dialogues En Francais*, is now available on Albany Records.

Bernhard was principal horn with The Saint Paul Chamber Orchestra where he was featured often as a soloist. In the SPCO he performed in Carnegie Hall, toured nationally, and internationally. He is a founding member of the Contrapunctus Brass Trio, a group whose mission is to help under-funded school music programs and to expand the brass chamber music repertoire. He has performed often with the Chicago Symphony, San Francisco Symphony, and the Minnesota Orchestra.

Bernhard has received awards from many other organizations such as The National Foundation for the Advancement in the Arts, and The Distinguished Music Alumni Award from the University of Wisconsin-Madison for outstanding artistry. In 2009 he became the first classical brass player to win Minnesota's prestigious McKnight Foundation Artist Fellowship.

He received his Bachelors Degree with honors from Northwestern University, Evanston, IL, and his Masters Degree at the University of Wisconsin–Madison where he was a Paul Collins Wisconsin Distinguished Fellow.

For more information about Bernhard, please visit his website at www.bernhardscully.com

Vincent Fuh, piano

Collaborative pianist Vincent Fuh received a Bachelor of Arts degree in piano performance from the University of Wisconsin-Madison. His primary experience came as a jazz pianist in Madison and Milwaukee, where he gained invaluable insight into the requirements of ensemble performance, before switching his focus to classical music. He is currently pianist with the Oakwood Chamber Players and has performed with Bach Dancing & Dynamite Society and the Madison Symphony Orchestra. Since 1998, Fuh has been pianist for Opera for the Young, a touring company that brings fully staged adaptations of operas to schools throughout the Midwest. Vincent stays active in popular music as pianist and composer/arranger for Madisalsa, a 10-piece salsa and latin jazz group, and El Clan Destino, a contemporary Afro-Cuban quartet that fuses elements of sacred and secular Cuban music with North American popular music. Expert in many styles of music, Vincent frequently performs cross-genre programs in multi-media installations, seeking to remove the boundaries between the world's musics